WOMEN WHO CHANGED THE WORLD

A FEMINIST BOOK FOR CHILDREN AGES 3–5

WOMEN WHO CHANGED THE WORLD

RACHELLE BURK

ROCKRIDGE
PRESS

FOR MY SWEET AUNT RENEE —R.B.

First Rockridge Press hardcover edition 2022

Rockridge Press and the Rockridge Press logo are trademarks or registered trademarks of Callisto Media Inc. and/or its affiliates in the United States and other countries and may not be used without written permission.

For general information on our other products and services, please contact our Customer Care Department within the United States at (866) 744-2665, or outside the United States at (510) 253-0500.

Hardcover ISBN: 978-1-63878-171-4 | eBook ISBN: 978-1-68539-155-3

Manufactured in the United States of America

Interior and Cover Designer: Carlos Esparza
Art Producer: Samantha Ulban
Editor: Elizabeth Baird
Production Editor: Jael Fogle
Production Manager: Lanore Coloprisco

Illustrations by © Lindsay Dale Scott, cover and pp.7-9, 28-30; © Ana Sanfelippo, cover and pp. 10-12 and 16-18; © Micah Player, cover and pp. 25-27; © Aura Lewis, cover and pp. 40-42; Collaborate Agency, pp. 1-3; © Loris Lora, pp. 4-6; © Pearl Law, pp. 13-15; © Sawyer Cloud, pp. 19-21; © Juanita Londoño, pp. 31-36; © Steffi Walthall, pp. 37-39.

10 9 8 7 6 5 4 3 2 1 0

CONTENTS

MEET SUSAN B. ANTHONY!

Susan was born at a time when many African Americans were enslaved and women could not vote. She thought these things were unfair. She believed that all people should be treated equally.

Susan helped enslaved people escape to freedom. During the Civil War, she formed a women's group that fought to end slavery. They held meetings, created petitions, and made speeches. After the war, new laws gave all African Americans their freedom and many rights.

Susan had more work to do. She became a leader of the suffragists, who fought for women's equality. Thanks to Susan and many other suffragists, American women won the right to vote in 1920.

MEET HARRIET TUBMAN!

Born into slavery, Harriet worked hard from morning till night. Her enslavers treated her and the other enslaved people cruelly. Harriet decided to escape. It would be dangerous, but Harriet was determined.

Freedom at last! When Harriet was safe in the north, she helped others escape slavery, too. Over the next few years, Harriet risked her life to lead more than seventy people to freedom.

Throughout her life, Harriet continued to bravely serve others. She was a nurse and a spy during the Civil War, and she helped fight for women's right to vote. Harriet was a hero to many!

MEET MARIE CURIE!

Marie wanted to be a scientist. In Poland, where she lived, women were not allowed to study science. So, she moved to France and got a job to pay for school.

Marie finally became a scientist and studied radiation. If you've ever had an X-ray, you can thank Marie for making this life-saving test possible. Because of her discoveries, doctors figured out that radiation could also treat cancer.

Marie was the first woman to win a Nobel Prize in Physics. She also won the Nobel Prize in Chemistry, becoming the only woman to ever win two Nobel Prizes!

MEET HELEN KELLER!

Helen lost her sight and hearing when she got sick as a baby. Her parents wondered if she would ever be able to learn or speak. They hired Anne Sullivan, who was also nearly blind, to teach Helen.

With Anne's help, Helen finally learned how to communicate. She learned to speak with her hands and read braille, a type of writing that uses raised dots on paper. She even learned to speak with her voice! She said her first words out loud at age nine: "It is too warm."

Helen became the first deaf and blind person to graduate from college. Helen believed that all people should be treated with respect and have the same opportunities. She spent her life fighting for the rights of women and people with disabilities.

MEET AMELIA EARHART!

As a child, Amelia loved adventure. She wanted to become a pilot, even though many people believed only men should be pilots. Amelia saved her money for flying lessons and then bought her own plane.

13

Soon, Amelia flew higher, faster, and farther than any female pilot ever had. She became the second person—and the first woman—to fly alone across the ocean. Sadly, when Amelia tried to become the first person to fly around the world, her plane mysteriously disappeared.

During her life, Amelia encouraged more women to become pilots. She even helped start a flying club for women called the Ninety-Nines, named after the number of founding members. Today, many women love to fly planes!

MEET FRIDA KAHLO!

F rida always enjoyed art. As a child in Mexico, both sickness and injury caused her pain that lasted all her life. Painting pictures helped Frida forget about her pain and express herself.

Frida had her own special style of painting, and was especially good at self-portraits. She created bright, colorful pictures with Mexican themes, animals, and nature. She was proud of her Mexican culture.

During Frida's lifetime, most famous artists were men. But now her paintings are in museums in many countries. Frida's art is celebrated all over the world.

MEET ELLA FITZGERALD!

Ella had a difficult childhood. Her mother died when she was young, and she was homeless for a time. Music helped her deal with her troubles. Sometimes she sang on street corners to earn money. As a teenager, Ella entered a talent contest at the famous Apollo Theater and won!

Soon, Ella became the first Black woman hired to sing in a famous jazz band, Chick Webb and His Orchestra. Ella toured with her band all over the world. She had a voice like a musical instrument that could glide easily between very high and very low notes.

Ella was the first Black woman to win a Grammy Award. She won thirteen Grammys and sold over forty million albums during her amazing career. Everyone calls Ella the Queen of Jazz!

MEET KATHERINE JOHNSON!

From a young age, Katherine excelled at math. She was so smart that she graduated high school when she was only fourteen. Later, she became one of the first Black students at West Virginia University, where she studied mathematics.

Katherine was one of the first Black women hired at NASA, the American space agency. Her math skills helped send the first astronauts into space—and get them back to Earth safely. Women did not usually attend meetings at NASA, but Katherine was so important that she was invited to lots of them.

Katherine helped the first astronauts land on the moon. She received many awards for her brilliant work, including the Presidential Medal of Freedom. This is a special award given to people who have made the United States a better place to live. Katherine shined like a star!

MEET RUTH BADER GINSBURG!

Ruth grew up during a time when women did not have many career choices. She wanted to change that. She believed women and men should have the same rights and opportunities.

Ruth went to law school. She was one of the
only women in her class. When she became a
lawyer, Ruth fought for women to be treated
the same as men.

The president of the United States gave Ruth an important job: Supreme Court justice! When people disagreed about laws, she listened to all sides. Ruth made big decisions so that all people were treated fairly, no matter who they were or where they were from.

MEET JANE GOODALL!

Growing up, Jane loved animals, especially her stuffed chimpanzee. When she was older, she saved up enough money to travel to Africa. There, she got a job studying real chimpanzees. Few women had jobs in this field.

The chimpanzees became almost like family to Jane. She watched and learned from them for over forty years. Jane saw that they felt emotions like happiness, sadness, and anger. She also discovered that they used tools like people do!

Jane's research has taught us more about chimpanzees than that of any other scientist in the world. She still works to protect chimpanzees and their habitat.

MEET KAMALA HARRIS!

Kamala's mother came to America from India, and her father from Jamaica. They taught Kamala that all Americans should be treated equally, no matter where they came from. She became a lawyer, helping women get better pay and keeping children safe.

31

Kamala was the first woman and the first person of color to be elected as California's top attorney. Later, she became a senator because she wanted to make new and better laws.

Kamala ran for vice president of the United States and won! As the first woman, first Black person, and first South Asian person to hold this office, she is a role model for many.

MEET MISTY COPELAND!

As a little girl, family problems sometimes made Misty sad. Dancing and performing always made her feel better. When she was thirteen, Misty took her first ballet class. Most ballerinas start dancing when they're very young, but Misty was so talented that she caught up quickly.

Soon, Misty knew she wanted to be a professional
ballet dancer. The ballet companies made this
hard for her. They wanted all the ballerinas
to look alike. Misty's skin color made her look
different from all the other professional dancers.
That did not stop her from dancing to the top!

Misty was the first Black woman to become a principal dancer for the American Ballet Theatre. She is determined that children of different backgrounds get the chance to become ballet dancers like her.

MEET SIMONE BILES!

As a little girl, Simone loved to bounce and flip. Gymnastics was the perfect sport for her. Simone spent so much time practicing that she had little time for friends and school activities.

Her dedication paid off. Simone competed all over the world, winning many awards. She even performed new gymnastics moves that no woman (and few men) had ever tried. Four of these moves were named after her. Finally, Simone made it to the Olympics!

Simone won more medals than any gymnast in history. But she believes that winning isn't everything. Today she helps athletes understand that it's also important to take care of your health and know when to rest. Simone is a real winner!

MEET MALALA YOUSAFZAI!

When Malala was growing up in Pakistan, girls were not allowed to go to school. Malala felt this wasn't fair. She loved school, so she broke the rules and went anyway.

40

Malala fought bravely, speaking out for girls' rights to an education. Soon, it became dangerous. The Taliban government tried to stop her.

Malala had to leave her country to continue her fight. She gave a speech to the United Nations about wanting all the world's children to get an education. For her courage and hard work, Malala became the youngest person ever to win a Nobel Peace Prize!

ABOUT THE AUTHOR

Rachelle Burk writes fiction and nonfiction for ages 2 to 12. Her other Rockridge Press titles include *The Story of Simone Biles, Stomp, Wiggle, Clap, and Tap: My First Book of Dance*, and *Let's Play an Instrument: A Music Book for Kids*. She visits elementary schools and preschools with her dynamic author visit programs. Visit her on the web at Rachelleburk.com.